Good Women in Bad Situations

And the Grace That Awaits Them

By Beverly D. Allen

PRESS

Thanks For Attending
CPC's
Women In Red
2012

Peace & Blessings
Sister Bessie

Love,
Evang Bessie Allen
2-18-12

Joel 2:13
And rend your heart and not your garments.
Now return to the Lord your God
For He is gracious and compassionate,
Slow to anger, abounding in lovingkindness
and relenting of evil.

Hebrews 4:16
Therefore let us draw near with confidence to the
throne of grace, so that we may receive
mercy and find grace to help in time
of need.

Dedication

I dedicate this book first to the Lord Jesus Christ with thanksgiving for His amazing grace, which met me and still meets me, and for the inspiration for this book. Secondly, to the memory of my wonderful mother, affectionately known as Mother Juliette Caldwell, whose words and encouragement continue to speak to me.

Acknowledgments

I want to first say thank you to my loving covenant partner and friend, Bishop Joseph Allen, for his faith in what God assigns me to do and his full support. I also want to thank my loving family members, who gave technical support, editorial comments, spiritual encouragement, and all I needed to help complete this labor of love. So thank you, Marc and Odette Allen, Sandra Gillead, Sonya Caldwell, and Carolyn Caldwell. I want to thank my dear friend Victoria Ufondu for the illustrations throughout this book. I cannot thank you all enough, but I pray that the Lord will thank you more properly for your sacrifices and the lending of your talents and gifts.

Contents

Preface

Good Women in Bad Situations...
And the Grace that Awaits Them

This awesome presentation of God's inspired word is masterfully written by Evangelist Beverly Allen to enlighten, inspire, motivate, and encourage women of all age groups to embrace one another with loving compassion through life's intrinsic journey. From the onset of these insightful vignettes that reveal the mental anguish of the "sisters" referenced herein; each is subsequently vindicated by virtue of their belief, trust, and conviction in knowing and/or discovering the all sufficiency of God's magnanimous grace.

As the dynamic persona of each testimony is illuminated through the pages of this book, we (as observers) are immediately thrust into a catechism of self-reflection which requires both an introspective look at who we are in the mind's eye of God; and subsequently a retrospective glance at God's grace, mercy, and favor as they are delivered from situations, circumstances, and events where feelings of dysfunction, abandonment, frustration, isolation, and perhaps even a sense of unworthiness had prevailed. Notwithstanding their intriguing pathways, the scope and sequence of Evangelist Allen's latest publication follows the pure essence of God's directive to mankind to: "be fruitful and multiply."

Through the annals of this text she ignites a pronounced urgency for the reader to recognize that God is elevating the landscape for His chosen vessels to transcend the boundaries of mediocrity to quintessential plateaus of excellence for His glory. Premiere illustrations of God's flawless plan for women captured by Evangelist Beverly Allen evokes an undeniable consciousness for women to be liberated so that they may be beacons of light radiating and encapsulating the infinite love of God.

Good Women in Bad Situations will affirm in your spirit the divine wisdom of God concerning you. Moreover, your anticipated transformation will yield great opportunities to help other women recognize through you the *Grace that Awaits Them* in their life's journey. Read, study, and be blessed for herein is your moment for reconciliation and restoration.

Dr. Stephaine Arrington, President

Interdenominational Women's Conference

Paterson, New Jersey

Foreword

Aline in one of my all-time favorite "chick flicks" haunts me to this day. The movie is *How to Make an American Quilt,* and the character Constance (Kate Nelligan) is telling the young protagonist, Finn (Winona Ryder), her story: "I think the hardest part of being a woman is having women friends," she says as she delves into her shameful past. Finn is captivated by this powerful opening line, and so are we.

Though bittersweet, a mound of truth is contained in that statement. We as women can be our own worst enemies, even when we call ourselves Christians. How many times have you caught yourself reveling in another woman's misfortunes, or secretly gloating when you watched her once-svelte figure pack on a few pounds? Men compete openly, whether in athletic prowess, military strategy, or corporate/

intellectual muscle. We, however, are much more subtle, wielding covert weapons of double-talk, passive aggression, and catty manipulation.

It is this tendency—which often boils down to a competition for the approval and admiration of *men*—that leads so many women to disparage her sisters, vying to improve their own status by demeaning others. But as the apostle Paul would say, *"God forbid!"* Were we not saved for more than this? Were we not redeemed *as women* to demonstrate to a watching world and to our sisters in Christ the love that comes from above?

> What shall we say then? Shall we continue in sin, that grace may abound? God forbid. How shall we, that are dead to sin, live any longer therein?

> Romans 6:1-2

Indeed, God has called us to be like Christ in our behavior toward our fellow females in the human race. This is the spirit behind *Good Women in Bad Situations,* in which author Beverly D. Allen appeals for us to "judge not" as we encounter real women whose lives mirror those of Bathsheba,

Rahab, Tamar, Michal, and other women in the Bible. Some of these biblical heroines found happy endings to their troubling stories; others became famous for being "infamous"— and their names still bear a scourge to this day.

As you read through the accounts of these women on the following pages, ask the Holy Spirit to plant seeds of love, gentleness, and forbearance in your heart so that the next time you encounter a woman who is trapped in sin, you will be a vessel of blessing rather than a conduit of condemnation. Who knows? You may be privileged to help her make a life-changing turn toward the Father.

A. J. Kiesling
Author, *Skizzer* and *Where Have All the Good Men Gone?*

Introduction

The headlines in 2008 reported multiple scandals of politicians and religious leaders caught in embarrassing situations that caused family shame and spousal distrust. When journalists scurried for interviews to get the scoop on all the sordid details, often the women implicated—accused of affairs with notable men married with children and respectable wives—proclaimed that they were not bad people. Those who heard the interview might ask how any of these women could knowingly commit such promiscuous acts with these prominent men, be caught, and yet claim their own goodness. Their acts, with those who proclaimed publicly their integrity and decency while holding their elected office or religious leadership position, are undeniably sinful—unrighteous, scandalous, perverted, even criminal in some points. But they are not totally bad people. They are like all of us: good people with a fallen nature who do bad things and make bad decisions, yet are capable of doing good and being kind.

When we do not understand how we were created and what we have become through our first parents, Adam and Eve, we always try to justify ourselves when we do wrong and convince others of our goodness, even when we hurt others. Many women never forgive themselves for past mistakes and poor decisions, which have cost them over a period of time. Countless situations shape our lives and influence our decision-making process, but in our judgment of others we do not often consider what brings those we condemn to make bad decisions and shameful mistakes which often cost families, children, other women, other men, and themselves great pain and even death.

The church at large is quick to condemn though we may not have all the information, and sometimes even with full information we are quicker not to forgive. But Jesus calls us to higher levels of forgiveness and reconciliation. We cannot afford to lose our compassion for the weak and the lost, for we are all weak in different areas of our lives. So much healing is needed in the church and in our communities, particularly if we are going to do true evangelism. Forgiveness, compassion, and reconciliation do not mean we condone evil or excuse sin. When the religious leaders—who had not publicly been caught in their own acts of wrongness—brought the woman caught in adultery to Jesus, He did not condemn her though He knew her sinful past. After He finished challenging those who were without sin to throw the first stone of judgment, He told the woman to "go and sin no more."

Most women don't get through life without making at least one bad decision that costs them some pain. Yours truly included!

CHAPTER ONE

BATHSHEBA'S SITUATION
(2Samuel 11:1-27; 12:1-23)

-A rendezvous with the king

-A wife's infidelity and her husband's murder

- The cover-up

BATHSHEBA was from a God-fearing family and the daughter of one of the king's high-ranking soldiers, Eliam or Ammiah, the son of Ahithopel. Eliam, whose name means "God is gracious," was one of David's gallant officers. She became the wife of Uriah, the most loyal of David's men. She was a woman who had great family credentials, a good woman we would call her, and yet she had a dirty secret that became very public because God exposed her and her lover, King David. This biblical account of her situation teaches us much about the tragedy of sin with its consequences and the power of God's forgiveness.

In 1 Kings 15:5 we read the record that "David did that which was right in the eyes of the Lord, and turned not aside from anything that he commanded him all the days of his life, save only in the matter of Uriah." While this may be the only blot on David's life story in serving Jehovah, it was a heavily engrained one, inerasable. This record shows us that while God freely pardons a sinner, the effects of sin remain. But it also shows us David's recognition of his sin and deep repentance for it, for he threw himself on the mercy of God. He did not waste time trying to justify why he did it or lie his way out of it, just because he was king. We do not have many words from Bathsheba describing her feelings in all of this, except her sending word to King David that she was pregnant (2 Samuel 11:5), "The woman conceived; and she sent and told David, and said, 'I am pregnant.'"

Before we condemn Bathsheba as a bad woman, let's look at what took place. A king weary of battles sent his men out to conquer Israel's enemies, led by his leading captain, Joab, the son of Ammon and Rabbah. He stayed home in Jerusalem. The ark of God was with the soldiers in the field, while David was at home in leisure (2 Samuel 11:11). The symbol and constant reminder of God's presence was separated from David long enough for him to do the unthinkable and cause this woman to have her good name tarnished. The tent housing the ark of the covenant would have been spotted and perhaps caused David to have some conviction, but its absence seemed to have no effect on him, or perhaps their behavior was the effect of its absence.

One very hot night Bathsheba was on the rooftop bathing, not unusual in Jerusalem's extreme heat, and she was probably "purifying herself from her uncleanness" or her menstrual cycle (Leviticus 15:19-24). The rooftop at night was a much cooler place, in the absence of a Jacuzzi. With David no longer fighting the battles of the Lord along with his men, he now sat back and took it easy, leaving himself open to attacks of his flesh and temptations. The enemy, the devil, is always looking for an opening to thwart the plans of God. Little does he know that the plans of God can never be thwarted. David saw a beautiful woman on the roof bathing at the same hour he went up to get some fresh cool air. He inquired who she was and found out she was the daughter of one of his main soldiers and the wife of one of his most loyal men. But he liked what he saw, and lust gripped his heart.

Neither David nor Bathsheba knew what Dr. Helen Fisher tells us in her book *Why We Love*. There are three mating drives in all humans: lust, romantic love, and attachment. Dr. Fisher says,

Very important, all of the basic drives are associated with elevated levels of central dopamine. So is romantic love. And like all the other drives, romantic love is a need, a craving. We need food. We need water. We need warmth. And the Lover feels he/she needs the beloved.[1]

Dr. Fisher has conducted research on the chemistry of love and reveals much about chemicals produced in the brain that drive us to physical attractions, whether based on love, lust, or obsessions. Dopamine is one such chemical, as Dr. Fisher explains:

Elevated levels of dopamine in the brain produce extremely focused attention, as well as unwavering motivation and goal-directed behavior. These are central characteristics of romantic love. Lovers intensely focus on the beloved, often to the exclusion of all around them. Indeed, they concentrate so relentlessly on the positive qualities of the adored one that they easily overlook his or her negative traits; they even dote on specific events and objects shared with this sweetheart.[2]

Dr. Fisher points out that dopamine is a strong stimulant which is persistent. She says:

In fact, dopamine may fuel the frantic effort a lover musters when he/she feels the love affair is in jeopardy. When a reward is delayed, dopamine-producing cells in the brain increase their work, pumping out more of this natural stimulant to energize the brain, focus attention, and drive the pursuer to strive even harder to acquire a reward: in this case, winning one's sweetheart.[3]

David and Bathsheba definitely had dopamine working in their brains, causing them to lose all restraints. Dr. Fisher points out "as dopamine increases in the brain, it often drives up levels of testosterone, the hormone of sexual desire."

Dr. Fisher explains how we function in nature, which helps us to understand how God designed us, but the Bible teaches that this design was created for a covenant relationship (1 Corinthians 7:2). All of these drives were to be activated with the one we commit to. In the absence of any godly principles and commitment, we will act as the worldly order dictates and condones.

The ark is away and two lonely, beautiful people are brought face-to-face. The scene is set. The king summons Bathsheba, probably to her surprise — perhaps thinking she is about to get bad news about her husband as she graces the palace of the king. David is described as a very good-looking young man and of good stature, meaning he must have had some build, ladies. The conversation went on into the night as the wine was poured and they drank. She must have been so impressed that the king was so taken with her that in time poor Uriah looked pretty weak compared to this king who was larger than life in Israel. We can judge her and condemn her, but remember there was no bad talk of her prior to this adulterous act. I imagine she was a good wife; she had no children. But the king had sent for her after he inquired about her. He had looked upon her too long; he wanted her and would have her, never thinking of the consequences or the cost to either of them. He did not think of his God, whom he worshipped and loved, for that moment. He was in a position of power, and power can be very seductive, as we have seen in our headlines when the president of the United States seduced a young intern. My, how we all condemned them. Yes, they were wrong. That behavior is never justified, but it can be understood when we understand the working of a sinful nature, with or without a commitment to Christ—which is why the Bible tells us not to judge others so quickly lest He judge us. The Bible tells us Bathsheba returned home after she purified herself from her uncleanness (2 Samuel 11:4). According to Leviticus 15:18, sexual intercourse required purification afterward.

They shared a blissful night together and David soon received news that he was going to be a daddy. This would disturb many things for them, because according to Leviticus 20:10 and Deuteronomy 22:22 they could be put to death. Yet, to add insult to injury, David tried to devise a strategy to bring Uriah home in the hope that he would sleep with his wife and take credit for Bathsheba's pregnancy. So, blinded by their sin when that didn't work, there was only one alternative—Uriah had to die to save them. In this act, Uriah was a type of Christ for them. As Christ, the sinless one died for the sinful, so Uriah the innocent one would die for their sin. As the record goes, Uriah was ordered to the front line so he would certainly be killed.

They thought they were safe until God sent the prophet Nathan to David to confront him with what he had done, in order that he might repent. Those of us who have ever been caught in sin and informed by God that we were not home free know the feeling of condemnation, the pain of failing God or failing those who had confidence in us and trusted us. Can you imagine the pain these two felt and their need for God's reconciliation, forgiveness, and love? This pain was not the only pain a holy, righteous, and just God would allow them to feel, for the baby they conceived in this adulterous act died (2 Samuel 12:15)—judgment for what they had done. The memory of that night would be relived over and over again, as well as the consequences for it.

STRENGTH FOR THIS SITUATION

Nathan told David all that would result from his secret sin, which was actually done in the sight of God.

Why have you despised the commandment of the Lord, to do evil in His sight?...For you did it secretly, but I will do this thing before all Israel, before the sun.

2 Samuel 12:9,12

It is amazing how the enemy blinds you and makes you feel that no one sees your sinful acts. He never prompts you to think that maybe God knows what is going on. But the Lord speaking through the prophet Nathan teaches us that God has eyes and ears to see and hear everything we do. The Bible tells us the eyes of the Lord go throughout the earth beholding good and evil. But sin will blind you every time. As God went to Adam to open his eyes, so God will come to us to show us our wrongdoings that we might repent and get back into fellowship with Him. Even if He has to chastise us to help us, He will, and chastisement does help us even if it is painful. In fact, it is because it is painful that we will often avoid the next opportunity to do a thing again.

Immediately after the pronouncement of God's judgment for their sin, David confesses to Nathan, "I have sinned against the Lord." David must have been cut to the heart, because he truly loved God, and Nathan must have witnessed his brokenness as well as God, for he gave David an assuring word,

The Lord also has put away your sin: you shall not die.

2 Samuel 12:13b

While this might have been of great comfort to David, the fact that his unborn child would be the one to die was not. Yet David knew that God is a God of mercy, and he sought mercy for his son with fasting in the temple after the child fell ill following his birth. David pleaded with God that the child might live and lay all night on the ground in the temple for seven days. On the seventh day the child died. David got up from the ground, washed and anointed himself, and went into the house of the Lord to worship.

This is a lesson on what to do when you sin and how to approach God. David knew that God was a God of compassion, mercy, forgiveness, and love. He never discounted the fact that God may change His mind. We should never try to state what God will do in the worst of situations. We should seek God and be willing to accept whatever judgment He proposes and worship Him still. For His judgments are righteous and He will have mercy on whom He will have mercy. This is another reason we can never judge others for their acts. We are called to be like God, slow to anger and full of compassion.

But here is the best encouragement for Bathsheba and David. No doubt, Bathsheba was deeply sorrowful at the loss of her baby. David had sought God on their behalf for the child, but the child still died. We are not told any conversation between the two of them on this matter. She must have wondered when David came to console her if God would be angry with them forever, and whether she would be able to have a good life again. Would God give them another chance, or would their relationship be rejected forever? Could there be life after adultery and murder for two people who were truly repentant?

God answers that question for them, because the Bible tells us David comforted Bathsheba, his wife, and went in to lay with her. I would imagine some time had lapsed, allowing her body to get back into order. But 2 Samuel 12:24-25 tells us that Bathsheba "conceived again" and bore a son, and David called him Solomon. "Now the Lord loved him, and He sent word by the hand of Nathan the prophet: So he called his name Jedidiah, because of the Lord." The name Jedidiah means "loved by the Lord." Solomon means "peace." David called this son peace because he felt the peace of God which passes all understanding after their utter failure before God.

I tell you God will give you peace because He loves you! God has not changed; He is still a God of love and mercy and forgiveness if you will repent.

LET'S NOT JUDGE TOO HARSHLY

Those of us who would condemn David and Bathsheba from the outset of hearing about their sin should hold off. While we don't condone what she did, we can have compassion for her. The Scriptures teach us this:

Brethren, if any man be overtaken in any trespass, you who are spiritual restore such a one in a spirit of gentleness, considering yourself lest you also be tempted.

Galatians 6:1

We know that what they did was wrong, but we do not know what drove them to do it, and before you blurt out sin remember that sin is the initiator of all evil we do. We tend to look only at the sin and not what drives anyone to commit certain sinful acts. For we all sin, but circumstances may drive each of us to act in different ways or make us more prone or vulnerable to certain sins. For instance, I do not know what type of relationship Uriah and Bathsheba had, but there were no children in this marriage. Perhaps they were both frustrated that their marriage had not produced any children. Uriah was a loyal soldier, but he may have been a poor husband. Perhaps they had an arranged marriage where no love was expressed. He may have been more loyal to his service than to a wife he owed much consideration.

Bathsheba was a beautiful woman, according to the Scriptures, but when her husband was brought home on leave, he would not go in to spend time with her. He would rather lie outside his home, choosing to be loyal to his troops, than sleep with his wife. There was nothing ungodly about being with his wife, whom he may not have seen for weeks. She had feelings he should have considered. Suppose he were to be killed? Most loving couples want to spend as much time with each other as possible, if the relationship is truly loving. What woman wants to send her husband off without displays of affection and intimacy? There may have been a host of reasons that caused Bathsheba to weaken to David's advances, beside the fact that David was very good-looking. We cannot rightly judge because we do not know the true story, which is why we cannot judge on the facts alone. God in His wisdom wants us to leave the judgment to Him, but He has given us the ministry of reconciliation (2 Corinthians 5:18).

When David summoned Bathsheba, we don't know if David made it difficult for her to say no—not suggesting rape, but he *was* the king of Israel. David was one of the most powerful men of her time, and he was taken with her, even if her husband may not have been. Yes, she could have and should have said no, but how many times have we not done what we could have and should have done in many situations?

When we rush to judge others, we are also judging ourselves. This does not mean we should not hate sin, it only means we have to differentiate between hating the sin and not hating the sinner. Any woman who has committed like sin as Bathsheba should not give up on life or herself. She should seek God's mercy and forgiveness and experience His love. Any judgment He assigns will be accompanied by His love and grace to endure it. He will still bless you in other areas of your life and in other ways. Bathsheba lost one son, but God gave her another, and we do not hear of any wrongdoing after that. In fact, she raised her son Solomon with godly diligence and care. Solomon reflects upon his mother's method of rearing him in Proverbs 22:6 when he writes, "Train up a child in the way he should go...."

Bathsheba's life teaches that, being assured of God's forgiveness, you do not need to let your past sins ruin your future. Scripture teaches that "if we confess our sins, He is faithful and just to forgive us our sins and to cleanse us from all unrighteousness" (1 John 1:9).

Bathsheba is in the line of the Messiah, and the Gospel of Matthew records her as such. Her son Solomon became the next king of Israel, as David's first wife was unable to bear children. This is one of the most encouraging accounts of a good woman in a bad situation and how when you take it to God, He will make good out of it if you trust Him. It is also another lesson not to judge and condemn people right away without offering any reconciliation or help to restore them back to God—or be a connection for someone to get to God who does not know Him.

There is strength in turning to God in every situation, and we learn this as we continue to see His hand in the lives of other good women in bad situations.

CHAPTER TWO

RAHAB'S SITUATION
(Joshua 2:1-22)

-Born into a heathen and idolatrous culture

-Prostitute and innkeeper

-Knowing when opportunity knocks

RAHAB "the harlot" was an Amorite from an idol-atrous people and family. The name "Ra" was the name of an Egyptian god. Her name meant insolence, fierceness, broad, spaciousness. She was a sinful woman whose sins were blatant and public, for her profession was not done in a corner. She had a place of business from which she conducted her services, apart from her parent's house. Three times over Rahab is referred to as "the harlot," and the Hebrew term *zoonah* and the Greek word *porne* have at no time meant anything else but "harlot," a woman who yields herself indiscriminately to every man approaching her.[1]

This is worthy of note because there are both Jewish and Christian writers who attempt to prove there is another Rahab who is not "the harlot" because her name is mentioned in the genealogy of Christ and by the apostle Paul as a woman of faith. They propose that a sinful woman such as Rahab is incapable of any human goodness. Every human being is capable of both good and evil. Even those of us who have been born again are capable of doing evil, as Paul said. When we seek to do good, evil is always present. Sometimes we succumb to evil and at other times we overcome it. Others suggest that "harlot" can be translated "innkeeper," which would identify Rahab as the owner of a wayside tavern. At any rate the Bible does not try to smooth over the unpleasant and disgraceful fact that Rahab had been a harlot as her occupation. There were not many occupations for women in those times, the highest and best being a wife and mother.

Although Rahab lived apart from her parents and siblings, she never lost her love and concern for her family. Her life-style may have been a means of support for her family. Some studies of occupations in that day indicate that prostitution may not have been regarded with the same horror then as it is now. After all, this was Jericho, a place where fertility worship was practiced. But the Bible repeatedly portrays harlotry with moral revulsion and social ostracism. However, it never regards the person who performs such acts as unre-deemable. In fact, this account of Rahab shows how God can despise and condemn the act, yet love the individual and cause a change in her life.

Rahab's courage and sacrifice demonstrate how a person may be in sin and not want to stay there. Some circumstances throw a person into survival mode for the present situation. We want to see the bigger picture—the position of the heart, not just the position of the harlot. Her occupation characterizes her as a no-good woman, trash, and not worthy of the best life can offer by moralists and self-righteous religious people. But we shall see how a woman's heart can be hidden until given the right opportunity to make a change. Sometimes the opportunity comes with pain and challenges, but when God is sought, there is enough enabling grace to encourage you to take hold of the opportunities.

A shameful past leaves most women with not only low self-esteem but self-condemnation and guilt. These in turn make a woman believe she does not deserve the best life has to offer, that she should take whatever she can get and be satisfied. God shows us through this biblical account how man may look on the outward appearance, but God looks on the heart. God saw what Rahab truly desired. It was not coincidence that brought the spies to Rahab's house but divine providence. God was showing Rahab she had another option!

Her desire for another way of life may have developed from hearing about a holy God from some of the travelers she entertained and sinned with, who gave the facts of the Exodus and the miracles He wrought toward His people Israel. Her house was the talk of the town, a main stopping post for the traveling merchants who came from out of town.

Rahab's house was built against the town wall with the roof almost level with the ramparts, and with a stairway leading up to a flat roof that appears to be a continuation of the wall. It was a logical place for the spies to go and gather information about Jericho. The spies stood out from all those in the town and were seen going into Rahab's house, for Joshua 2:2-7 tells how the king of Jericho got word of their arrival and sent to Rahab's house to have the spies brought to him. Their plot was discovered, and Rahab had to make a quick decision, for the opportunity for change was knocking. If she had been in love with her lifestyle, all she had to do was turn over the spies to the officials. But she seized the moment and by faith took courage and hid the spies on the rooftop under stalks of flax. When asked, she threw the searching officials off and told them the spies had been there but left right before the closing of the city gates, and they could catch up with them if they hurried. She said to the spies, "I know that the Lord has given you the land, and that the fear of you has fallen upon us, and that all the inhabitants of the land melt away before you" (Joshua 2:8-14).

After sharing with them all she had heard about their God and what He did for His people, she asked them to deal kindly with her and her family when they came back to take the city. Late that night she lowered the spies out the window on a scarlet rope to the ground and instructed them to escape to the hills and stay there for three days so the pursuers would give up believing they had gotten away. The spies would have been put to death if caught, but thanks to Rahab's quick thinking and desire to be saved, she trusted in the God of Israel and believed He would deliver her if she protected the spies. What faith this demonstrated.

Rahab had grown up in Jericho and was part of the culture and religious worship there all her life, along with her parents and siblings. She could have been killed for treason if discovered helping the spies, but it was her one chance to make a change. God had sent her this opportunity to make a life change. The God of Israel knew her heart apart from all the people in that city, just as He knew the number of those in Sodom and Gomorrah who were righteous. While she was labeled a harlot, she was still a good woman who may not have chosen the best profession but wanted to be saved along with her family and was willing to risk her life. When she sold out her nation in exchange for her deliverance from Jericho, she was giving up the Canaanite lifestyle and all associated with it. This included child sacrifice— saving her future offspring—and fertility worship with its sexual perversion. No more entertaining strangers who came to town; perhaps she could settle down and have a normal life. What would God have in store for her, a former harlot? What could she expect now that everyone would know what her former life was at the word of the spies? She would soon find out. The same scarlet rope that saved the spies was the symbol they would see to spare her house when they swept through the city destroying the inhabitants of Jericho. This rope was like the blood upon the doorposts in Egypt, a sign that God was covering this house. She and her family were safely delivered as the spies had promised.

Deliverance was not the only reward God had for this harlot. Now she would become a part of this new community and adapt to their culture and worship of the one true and living God. Her adoption by this people and their God would usher in the blessings that come along with serving Him. A woman with a past like Rahab's might feel awkward around those who were against everything her people believed, a people with commandments from the hand of God and animal sacrifices for sins. She may have wished she had been born to this people and brought up under their God, especially in light of her past life when measured next to theirs. How could she comprehend the forgiveness and grace of God unless she could experience it in a very personal way? She did not know that what she did was sin until she came in contact with a new way of life and a very different way to worship God. What God was about to do would allow her to have this experience, for the spy she helped save would be the man God gave her as a husband. Salmon was a prince in Israel, a very courageous man who knew her and her past and was predestined to be in the lineage of the Messiah. Out of all the daughters born at this time, even within Israel, she would be the one to marry this fine young man. What a lesson to learn about God, one He desires us to know and believe! "He that cometh to God must believe that He is and that He is a rewarder of them that diligently seek Him" (Hebrews 11:6). Rahab's faith saved her according to Hebrew 11:31:

By faith the harlot Rahab did not perish with those who did not believe, when she had received the spies with peace.

The Gospel of Matthew includes her in the genealogy of Jesus, raising her status by being linked to the Messiah through her seed, Boaz.

RAHAB'S PLIGHT

There were not many occupations a woman could take up in most ancient cultures. The place of women was very low, and as paganism developed their social condition went backward. Polygamy, which was a common practice, was degrading for women and cheapened womanhood, and the Scriptures show us how it brought about much animosity and separation (Genesis 21:32; 1 Kings 2:19; 7:8; 15:13; Esther 2:3, 9). The numerous cults of Oriental paganism caused women to suffer enslavement and debasement. Under Mohammedism, women became degraded, endured rigid seclusion, were shut out of ordinary society, and forced to conceal their features in any public place. Israelite women, however, went about with their faces exposed to public view, the veil being used on certain occasions (Genesis 12:14; 24:64, 65; 29:10, 11; 38:14). In Assyria a man could mock his wife and say to her, "Thou are not my wife," which freed him from her. If a woman repudiated her husband, she could be drowned. Under Roman law, the woman had little freedom. On her marriage her property became her husband's, and all her earnings were his. Christianity, however, restored women's rights and also the sacredness of marriage.[2]

I gave this background information to help us understand Rahab's plight in Jericho. We could rush to judge her wrongly, as we do others, without trying to see the bigger picture or what may motivate any woman to do things that seem so horrible. Rahab obviously loved her family, for she interceded for them as well, which makes her a good woman. If we are honest, we know that while we see ourselves as good women, we have done things we do not want exposed to anyone. Yet, if we are good how can we do bad things? The answer is because of our inherited sinful nature, which is not always controlled by the Spirit of God. When we truly understand this, we will not rush to judge the Rahabs of the world but find a way through the love of

Christ to reach out to them. We will see the need to help lift them from their sin and love them as Christ loves them, all at the same time.

If God did this for Rahab, it proves the Scriptures right: "Therefore, if anyone is in Christ, he is a new creation; old things have passed away; behold, all things have become new" (2 Corinthians 5:17). Now for those who already know Christ and have fallen short again of His glory, the Scriptures proclaim, "If we confess our sins, He is faithful and just to forgive us our sins and to cleanse us from all unrighteousness" (1 John 1:9). Far too many women are being held hostage over mistakes they have made and still make from time to time, trying to live a life that is pleasing to God and unable to be honest with those who are "spiritual" for fear of harsh judgment without any reconciliation. They really want to tell someone, for their conscience and their spirit have convicted them—praise God! But we are not compassionate enough at times to help loose them from the enemy's grip that keeps them in bondage.

Well, God's treatment of Rahab is a lesson for any woman who has fallen short and wants reconciliation and restoration. When you can't find anyone to reconcile you to God, trust the Word of God and believe that when you repent and confess your sins, God will forgive you and restore your fellowship with Him. If you never had it and want it, He will give it to you now.

CHAPTER THREE

TAMAR'S SITUATION
(Genesis 38:1-30)

-Husband dies and no children

-Needs a baby daddy

- Second husband dies and no children

-A father-in-law for a surrogate father by way of deception

T AMAR married into the family of Judah, which brought heartache and tragedy. She was a Canaanite, and marriages to Canaanites were not proudly looked upon or encouraged (Genesis 24:3, 26:34-35, 28:1). Judah, a son of Jacob or Israel, was a respectable family for according to prophecy and Scripture the Messiah would come from this tribe. Tamar hailed from a people who were the opposite of those a holy God was developing. They were polytheistic, practiced child sacrifice, and engaged in sensual and perverted fertility worship. The fact that Judah helped arrange Er's marriage to Tamar demonstrates his own spiritual weakness and disobedience to the instructions handed down from Abraham, Isaac, and Jacob.

Er did not have a long life with Tamar, for the Bible tells us he "was wicked in the sight of the Lord, and the Lord put him to death" (Genesis 38:6 ESV). Now the Levirate law in Deuteronomy 25:5-10 says that the deceased's unmarried brother is obliged to marry his brother's widow and raise up children in the name of his brother so that his name will not be blotted out of Israel. Judah had another son, Onan, whom he gave to Tamar to fulfill this law. But Onan was not happy about having offspring with Tamar that could not be his, so he performed what is known as *coitus interruptus* or "Onanism" every time he went in to his brother's wife. He would have a climax but withdraw before the semen could be transferred to Tamar; he spilled it on the ground. He publicly fulfilled his father's request but would rather let his precious seed fall to the ground and die than give life in his dead brother's name. How selfish and wicked this was in the sight of the Lord. So God put him to death (Genesis 38:10).

Now, what Tamar was about to do will seem disgusting to us, but to a Canaanite woman and a woman desperate to have children and a husband, which her future rested on, this was a serious problem. There were no retirement programs for women who could not work. A husband, and children who would take care of you should your spouse die, was the only prospect for survival. Of course you could sell yourself into slavery or perhaps be a concubine as some women were. Judah had another younger son, Shelah, who at the time was too young to marry Tamar. So Judah told Tamar to go back to stay with her father until Shelah came of age. He treated Tamar as if she were dangerous when it was actually his two sons who had done evil in the sight of the Lord and caused their own deaths. But the Scriptures indicate that in time Judah's wife died, and he went up to Timnah with his sheepshearers to be comforted along with his friend Hirah the Adullamite.

Tamar heard that her father-in-law was going up to Timnah to shear his sheep, so she took off her widow's garments, covered herself with a veil, wrapped herself up, and sat at the entrance to Enaim, the road to Timnah. She had seen that Shelah had grown up and was not given to her for marriage. The prospect of Shelah raising up seed for his deceased brother was over; Judah would not risk the death of his only remaining son, as if Tamar had caused his wicked sons' deaths like a bad luck charm. Perhaps he knew his son's rebellion to be like that of the other two who died. We do not know what type of father Judah was. He obviously was not devoted to the laws of his people made by the true and living

God. Judah extended his daughter-in-law a proposal to go in to her by the wayside, not recognizing who she was and mistaking her for a town prostitute. Tamar recognized Judah, and when he asked her to lay with him, she asked what he would give her in return. He said he would send her a young goat from his flock—love on credit, can you imagine? She was smart because she knew Judah was not a man of his word and therefore wanted him to give her his signet, cord, and staff in pledge—proof that he had been there with her in case he ever tried to deny it.

Judah kept his word to send back the young goat in exchange for the items he left as his pledge, but when his friend Hirah went looking for a prostitute who sat where Tamar was, he could not find her. Hirah returned to Judah and told him he could not find the woman to give her the goat, and the men of the place confirmed that no cult prostitute had been here. So Judah determined to let her keep the items as her own to avoid becoming the laughingstock of Timnah. Three months later Judah learned that his daughter-in-law was pregnant and had been immoral in doing so. After all, she was a widow and no marriage had taken place with Shelah or any other man. So Judah got on his self-righteous high horse, the man who only three months ago lay with a woman he thought was just a prostitute used to comfort him after his wife died. He went out of town to do his dirty deeds. But he called Tamar out and said, "Let her be burned" (Genesis 38:24). As Tamar was being brought out, however, she sent word to Judah that she was pregnant by the man whose articles she held. What a surprise Judah was in for! She asked him to identify the items, and seeing them put him to shame and prompted his admission that she was more righteous than he because he had not given his son as the law required. After that one act he never knew her again.

God's justice is amazing! Tamar, who had lost two husbands and had no children by either because of each one's wickedness, got a double blessing for she had twin boys, Zerah and Perez. Not only this, but Perez, the younger of the two, pushed his older brother Zerah aside and made an exit first to be the one that the lion of the tribe of Judah would come from, and the Davidic kingdom. Who would have believed a Canaanite woman, persistent to get blessed, would be in the lineage of the Messiah? Her deception was done through desperation and need; she had tried to do it the right way. The one who was supposed to be honest and keep the law was a poor witness and spiritually weak in that he did not trust God for his family's posterity.

TO JUDGE OR NOT TO JUDGE

As Judah rushed to judge Tamar before he had all the facts, so do we judge the Tamars of our society. We only know what we see and do not always get the full story. Even when we know the facts we cannot judge properly because we can't explain anyone's thoughts or motivations. We do not know the lifestyle, environment, or associations that shape people's thinking. All we can see are the sins, the tragedies and consequences. It is no wonder God tells us to leave judgment up to Him. Throughout the Bible we see God dealing with women in such a tender way, even when they make mistakes and become repentant and desire to change. Men look on the outward appearance, but God sees the heart.

There are far too many Tamars walking around in bondage because their life stories are attached to shame and disgrace. We think the Tamars are only lowlifes or heathen outcasts, but think again—many are from noble families, upper middle class, well educated, business entrepreneurs, CEOs, pastors, ministers, missionaries, lawyers, doctors, and many other walks of life that we have read about in our newspapers and seen on our newscasts. Is there no compassion and redemption for them? Is there no way to reach them before they commit suicide, resolving to give up on life? Bus stations are full of young women and men who ran away from home and got involved in modes of survival they are not proud of, sons and daughters who had relationships or took drugs that left them with irreversible physical ailments such as HIV and other STDs, which are spreading because of shame and hopelessness. We must be Christian enough to allow people to tell us what they are struggling with so their shame does not cause them to die in hopelessness and silence.

There is strength for each and every situation anyone faces. That strength is found in Jesus Christ. His opinion is far different from ours, for His ways are not our ways, neither are His thoughts our thoughts. His mercies are renewed every morning; He doesn't wake up angry over the same incidents every day. I believe God desires to use each of us who say we are Christian today as never before, because where sin abounds, grace does much more abound. We must be mirrors of His grace and transporters to those who can't find it or would never believe that it is for them.

CHAPTER FOUR

MICHAL'S SITUATION
(1Samuel 18:20-30)

- A princess used as a pawn for her father's purposes

- A young lovely wife forgotten by her husband and
solicited to another
man by her father

- Again used for political purposes by her husband to
officially gain the throne
of his people, being removed from the home of the man
her father joined her to.

-A bitter woman who has been tossed from one man to
another and from
one situation to another, never achieving any real
happiness

MICHAL is the daughter of King Saul, whom we meet in 1 Samuel 18:20: "Now Michal, Saul's daughter, loved David...." Saul had offered his older daughter, Merab, to the one who would slay Goliath the giant. Saul did not keep his promise but instead gave her to Adriel the Meholathite for a wife (vs. 19). This promise was now to be conditional on further military service, with the hope that David would be killed by an enemy and not by Saul himself. It was normal for a bride-price to be paid by the bridegroom to the father of the bride (Genesis 34:12; Exodus 22:16) as compensation for the loss of his daughter and insurance for her support if widowed. Instead, Saul required David to pass a test befitting a great warrior, hoping that he would fall. But God's favor was on David, revealed not in his military accomplishments alone but also in Michal's love for David. Well, we all know the rest of this story, how David slew Goliath and Saul gave Michal to David to be married (1 Samuel 18:27).

Saul's jealousy of David grew and he sought in many ways to destroy him secretly, but everything Saul planned to use against David turned to David's advantage. While the king feared David because the Lord's hand was evident upon him, he still had deeply rooted jealousy for him. This did not stop Michal from loving David deeply, so much so that when she found out that Saul was going to have him killed one night, she helped him escape, risking the love of her father (1 Samuel 19:11-17).

I believe Saul never forgave his daughter's deception for he gave her to be the wife of another man, Palti the son of Laish from Gallim (1 Samuel 25:44). This was against the laws of God, knowing that he was causing his daughter to commit adultery, for her husband was yet alive. We do not hear that Michal was happy or that she had children, or that she even loved Palti. We do see her some years later and about eight of David's wives later, who each had a son. At some point Michal raised her sister's five sons due to the untimely death of their mother, and what happens to these boys is another tragedy Michal had to deal with on top of everything else going on in her life.

What Michal seems to be most remembered for is her attitude at seeing her husband David dancing out of his royal garments, exuberant over the return of the ark of God back into the Israelites' midst.

> Then it happened as the ark of the Lord came into the city of David that Michal the daughter of Saul looked out of the window and saw King David leaping and dancing before the Lord; and she despised him in her heart.
>
> 2 Samuel 6:16

This scripture leads us to believe that Michal is a bad woman, perhaps spoiled and unappreciative of her royal upbringing and privileged life. I myself always read this and thought, *How could she feel this way about David just because he rejoiced over the ark of God being back with them?* The returning ark meant they had victory over their enemies and, more importantly, that the presence of God was with them.

We often see some women at their worst in a moment and judge their circumstances or their obvious attitude without knowing what caused a change in their temperament. Many a saint has judged Michal without trying to understand what could have caused her to go from loving David enough to sacrifice her relationship with her father for him to despising him.

Well, let's look a little closer at her journey. Her father gave her to David not because he wanted him as a son-in-law, but because he felt he had to fulfill his promise to David. He also felt that this association would allow him a position close enough to destroy David, not caring what it would mean to his daughter. Saul was no example to his daughter of a godly father. He used her to his own means with no regard for her feelings.

Because of her father, Michal's husband is a fugitive on the run from Saul and other enemies. He is separated from his wife but takes to himself seven other wives while separated from Michal. Certainly Michal heard about David's activities and the children he had with these other concubines (2 Samuel 3:1-5). By the way, one of the women he married was also a princess like her, the daughter of a king.

As if these wives were not enough we are told in 2 Samuel 5:13:

Meanwhile David took more concubines and wives from Jerusalem, after he came from Hebron; and more sons and daughters were born to David.

Keep in mind that these are in addition to the other seven wives and sons he already had while he was on the run from Saul, but Saul is now dead. We begin to see the journey of this once young, vibrant, in love princess who originally planned to be with David and have his children and enjoy a wonderful life together. But her dreams were destroyed by her father's jealousy and his backslidden condition. He was not committed to Jehovah as David was. Her husband fled her father's wrath, refusing to strike back at the Lord's anointed. He himself was on a journey. Her father married her off to someone else thinking the throne would be secure from David, not understanding that God had chosen him to be king and for that reason alone his attempts to keep David from it were useless. Her sister met an untimely death, and Michal was left to raise her five sons for whom she would suffer anguish when they were hung out to dry on a hill at

Gibeah, by the Gibeonites, as revenge for Saul's bloodthirsty zeal against them (2 Samuel 21:8).

David ceased to be on the run after Saul's death, and while he was unofficially king, he along with the ruling elders of Israel realized it would be more official if he showed himself as the son-in-law of Saul before all the people. So he made a deal with Abner, the captain of the armies of God's people, which included bringing Michal back to him. This unsettled her from her somewhat adjusted lifestyle with the man who had been her husband for a number of years.

Where had David been all this time? He had fought the Philistines and other enemies of his people. Why had he not fought even her father to bring Michal back to him or rescue her from the man her father tried to replace him with? Now, because he was about to be king, he wanted her back, with no regard for her new family and life. It was bad enough that her father used her for a pawn; now her first husband would do the same.

Which one of us women would not have been affected by all these circumstances? So much so that when we see David dancing before God over the ark, we wonder how one who always said he loved Jehovah so much could sleep with so many other women. He would mourn over enemies

74

coming into a village and taking the women and children. This incited anger in David such that he went to the enemy's camp and took back what they had stolen, wives and children. Yet he had not put up a fight to get back his first wife whom he had slain one hundred Philistines for, taking their foreskins off as proof of his worthiness to marry the king's daughter. How would this make Michal feel, or any woman for that matter?

All of that must have gone through Michal's mind while watching David dance before the Lord. Michal was a good woman in a bad situation. Reading Michal's plight should help us to understand or at least look a little closer at other women we come in contact with whose attitudes seem to be out of sorts. Before we judge them and call them bad women, we should know that even good women do bad things sometimes, which does not make them totally bad, as if there were no good in them. God made us good but sin twisted our nature, and we have knowledge of good and evil. Sometimes the good wins out and sometimes the evil, as Paul said. When he sought to do good, evil was always present. If only Michal had learned to love God wholly and allowed Him to use her knowing that all things work together for good. If only she could have had wise counsel. I do not hear of her having much to do with her mother. But learning all these things about her life helps to put her attitude in perspective. While I don't condone it, I do understand it. Now the Scriptures say she had no children till the day she died. This may have been a judgment from God, but it does not say that God shut up her womb. Perhaps her poor attitude did not allow a good relationship between her and David, and that was why she had no children. She was back in the palace but not back in the love relationship she formerly had with David.

Let us not judge the Michals of the world so harshly. Let us pray for them and if given the opportunity encourage them and help them to see God is able to turn the situation around if they are willing to forgive and allow Him to use all things that happen in their lives for good. Let us show them that they have a High Priest who can be touched with the feelings of their infirmities, and that He loves them with an everlasting love.

A LESSON LEARNED

There is a lesson to be learned from Michal. Bathsheba, whom David had an affair with and whose husband he killed to hide his sin, was judged and punished along with David, but they both repented and God blessed them despite what they did. He forgave them, and their son Solomon became the third king of Israel. Who knows what would have happened if when David sent for Michal, she had forgiven him and sought Jehovah for strength? She may have had children of her own, one who would be king. When we don't seek God in all our situations, we fail to receive the wisdom and divine guidance we so desperately need, and the healing only He can give. No matter what your situation is or has been, don't give up on God. Ask the Savior to help you, comfort you, strengthen you, and keep you. He is willing to aid you; He will carry you through!

CHAPTER FIVE

JEZEBEL'S SITUATION
(1 Kings 15:31 – 2 Kings 9:33-37)

- Raised in a perverted sensual religion from childhood devoted
to Baal and his worship

- Daughter of a king and priest who made her a female carbon copy of himself

- Married to one of Jehovah's weak, wicked kings who was backslidden from Jehovah

- Dominated her husband and children

- Feared by many because of her cold callousness—she feared no man or God

- Nurtured in an evil environment by an evil father, a cruel king and priest

- Trained to be devoted to her religion and gods, which promoted sexual rituals

- Married to a king who could have helped her but was wicked like her father and preferred the rituals of his wife's sensual worship

JEZABEL'S name meant chaste, free from carnal connection. Now someone may be saying, "Oh, please don't tell me you think Jezebel is a good woman." I am only trying to show how she may have become this woman so talked about as the most evil woman in the Bible—and understand her journey. Many writers say by nature she was a licentious woman, a wanton voluptuary. How did she go so far from the name her mother gave her at birth? She did not become perhaps what her mother dreamed she would be as a young princess, born into a royal family. Her father was King Ethbaal of the Zidonians and priest of Baal worshipers. The Zidonians came from a city in Phoenicia called Sidon and were also called Phoenicians.

The Phoenicians were a remarkable race, but they were idolators who regarded Jehovah as only a local deity, "the god of the land." Their gods were Baal and Ashtaroth, or Astarte, with their innumerable priests, 450 of whom Ahab installed in the magnificent temple to the Sun-god he built in Samaria. Another 400 priests were housed in a sanctuary Jezebel erected for them and which she fed at her own table.

Cruel and licentious rites were associated with the worship of Baal. Jezebel came from the same lineage that afterward produced the greatest soldier of antiquity. Jezebel's spirit of unforgiveness and daring rivaled even that of Hannibal with his notorious temper. While we see her in such a dark light from her historical account, we must consider her journey from her mother's breast to her husband Ahab.

We know very little about her mother, the queen. Historical records are silent, and no name is given. This could mean her mother died young after her birth. Her father could have had her killed or put away. But this is all speculation in the absence of any facts. Her mother may have hoped Jezebel would not be as her father or his religion would dictate, given her name. Her religion was carnal and connected to sexual rituals, and she was far from chaste as her name implied. Perhaps her mother knew the heartbreak of such a sensual religion—which catered to fertility gods— and hoped her daughter would have no part in that. But her father was not only the king but also the priest of the people and his household.

The Bible says to train up a child in the way he should go, and when he is old he will not depart from it. Jezebel was trained by her father's own lifestyle in their house, and he taught her everything about his gods. She was a loyal and devoted worshiper. She had absolute faith and trust in these gods. Jezebel's zeal for the worship of Ashtaroth was unmatched by any other in her father's kingdom. She secured the maintenance of hundreds of idolatrous priests.

This religious worship could only grow a cold hardened heart, which Jezebel had. Idol gods cannot produce what the true and living God can. Only Jesus can take away a stony heart and give one a heart of flesh. Her husband was too backslidden and far from God—to be expected since his own father was just as far from God, not giving his son a good example to follow.

If Jezebel had a husband devoted to Yahweh, or Jehovah, she would have had a chance, for she wanted to worship God but was indoctrinated to cold stone gods. Totally committed to her religion, what a witness she would have been if someone had demonstrated the power of the true and living God over Baal. But no one she was surrounded with had a relationship with Him. She was given example after example and space to repent, but her heart belonged to Baal.

How sad for this woman, who had so much potential, for she was one of God's creatures, and it was not His will that she should perish but that she should come to repentance. Her story is legendary in the Scriptures, and her name is synonymous with sin and evil. I believe she was a good woman placed in a bad situation from her early childhood. She was a product of her home and culture, which were ingrained in her. As well, her daughter, Athaliah, and sons, Ahaziah and Jehoram, were as wicked as their mother and father. It has been said that the "apples don't fall far from the tree," meaning that you cannot help but be affected by those you are closely associated with. Another adage states "association brings on assimilation." Their environment was totally wicked. King Ahab was from the stock of God's people Israel and their God, Jehovah. But he was not worshiping the true and living God, he was serving the god of his flesh, Baal. There was no one in Jezebel's circle who could witness to her. The victory of Jehovah through his prophet Elijah—

over Baal and all his prophets as the God who answered by fire—should have been a great enough witness for Jezebel. But she was so devoted to Baal that even God's miraculous victory on Mt. Carmel only angered her more against the prophet Elijah.

There are Jezebels in our society today in corporations, universities, courtrooms, hospitals, and homes. They have been so affected by their parents and their environment that only the help of those who are true believers—those who can be a witness and an example, a light to those who walk in darkness—can reverse the works of the enemy, Satan, in their lives. We must pray on their behalf if we truly want to see their souls saved.

Jezebel needs to be saved, and we must seek to win her to Christ. She probably appears hopelessly uninterested, but we must be instant in season and out of season. We must be compassionate and understanding without condoning her behavior. We must try to reach those who are perishing no matter how hopeless they seem to be.

We may not save Jezebel, but we must try and not prejudge her and say she does not want to be saved, passing her by. She needs to be saved, her children need to be saved, and her husband needs to be saved. Show Jezebel the love of

Christ which dwells in your heart as a believer. The Lord can save even Jezebel, for with God all things are possible. We must understand how Jezebel became who she turned out to be, which will make us compassionate and thankful to God for how He saved us despite our journey.

CHAPTER SIX

AN UNNAMED SINFUL WOMAN'S SITUATION
(Luke 7:36-50)

- A woman known for her sinful life

- Went as an uninvited guest to a strict
religious leader's home

- A humiliating announcement about her past

A SINFUL WOMAN, as this woman is referred to, points to the unchaste behavior she was known for among the people in the community—the sensual and hateful calling of a prostitute or woman of the streets. Luke alone of the four Gospels gives the account of this woman and her encounter with Jesus. Now all women since God created Eve, after she fell to sin, were born in sin and are sinners by birth, becoming sinners by practice. But this woman, whom Jesus met in Simon the Pharisee's house, is given the distinguishing labels "which was a sinner," "she is a sinner," and "her sins which were many."

This woman could be any woman, and writers have attempted to identify her as Mary Magdalene or Mary of Bethany. Jesus only refers to her as "this woman." No one was more sensitive to the pain of women as Jesus. This becomes clearer as we revisit this story. Jesus was invited to Simon the Pharisee's house, not because Simon admired Jesus or believed His teachings, but because Jesus was popular and could show that Simon had enough prestige to get His attention. It would also allow his fellow Pharisaic brethren to cross-examine Jesus to try and catch him in some legal breach of the law as given by Moses. Simon did not afford Him the Jewish rituals of hospitality given to those invited to one's home.

An outcast of a woman, though she was not invited in the usual manner, was allowed entrance — not stopped at the door. Simon knew who she was, but she had heard about Jesus going to the Pharisee's home to have dinner. She had heard Jesus' message of love and forgiveness. She had heard of His miraculous healings and listened to the tender words He spoke. It was all enough for her to conclude that He must be the Messiah, or at least He could help her make a change in her life. It would mean making herself vulnerable to those who did not approve of her, in fact hated her kind and did not want her to come to their house for fear she would pollute it. But her need outweighed her fears and cares about what others thought.

The sinful woman breaks into Simon's house and goes to Jesus' feet while He is reclining, having His meal. She sees that no sign of hospitality has been shown Him from the dust on His feet. No one offers her a basin of water to wash His feet or a towel to dry them or ointment to soothe them. But she came prepared. The thought of her past pain can produce water enough to wash His feet; her heart of repentance can barely stop the flow of tears once they start. She has enough hair to absorb the water from His feet to dry them. Her hair, used to seduce others and perhaps her greatest vanity, now is only good enough to wipe the wet dirt from His feet. The alabaster box she wears to perfume the beds she lies in now becomes a perfume offering to God and a healing method for dry, parched feet which had journeyed over the dusty roads of the city.

Jesus kept eating while the sinful woman attended to the pleasant courtesies not afforded Him by Simon. Simon dared not say anything, but he thought to himself that if Jesus was a real prophet He would never let such a woman touch Him. For who knew what disease she may be carrying, or what perverted motive she might have. He could not see what this woman saw in Jesus, the divine holiness of the Son of God, for he was too self-righteous and in need of nothing. She came to the house full of guilt and shame and would not even look Jesus in the eye, but only bow at His feet. But this woman took the most expensive item she had, her ointment—lavish and expensive, formerly for her clientele of men—and gave it to the purest of men. She was not so hardened by her sin that she was incapable of tears. Simon was just the opposite; he had a cold, calculated attitude of self-righteousness, which made him unsympathetic toward this woman's expression of gratitude and devotion.

Jesus knew Simon's thoughts and addressed them with a story about two debtors (Matthew 18:25). He said, "Simon, I have something to say to you." And he answered, "Say it, Teacher." Then Jesus told him of two debtors, one which owed five hundred denariis (twenty months' wages), and the other fifty (two months' wages).The moneylender forgave both their debts, so Jesus asked which one would love him more. Simon answered, "The one, I suppose, for whom he cancelled the larger debt." Well, he was right on this one. Then Jesus pointed to the sinful woman and said, "Her sins, which are many, are the reason she showed me the affection and kindness. When I entered your house, you did not extend to me the same courtesies you showed your other guests, but this woman did not cease to show her love and gratitude since entering your house." Simon was left to judge for himself the difference between this woman and him.

This is an even greater lesson for us who judge the many sins of others perhaps because we have forgotten what Jesus has done for us, how much He has delivered us from, not so long ago. Jesus was not ashamed to be touched by a woman who sinned much and was shunned by others. Neither is He afraid to be touched by any woman who has sinned much, who thinks she is too far away from God to receive His forgiveness and love. It does not matter where you have been or what you have done. The Bible says where there is much sin, there is much more grace.

Let us not forget this lesson to Simon and the Pharisees. Those who have been forgiven much will love much. They will love others who have sinned much too. Jesus constantly expressed His love and forgiveness for sinners. We need no further proof as to who can be forgiven or for how much they can be forgiven. All we need to do is take God at His Word and believe!

CHAPTER SEVEN

THE WOMAN OF SAMARIA'S SITUATION
(John 4:7-42)

- Poor and living in shame

- Five ex-husbands

- A new lover

The **SAMARITAN WOMAN'S** story has been revisited by many preachers and Bible teachers, and it bears reconsideration at this time for the sake of seeing God's response and treatment of such a woman. This woman was raised up under a great hostility that existed between Jews and Samaritans. The origin of their hostility is traced back to the Assyrian colonization of the land of Israel (2 Kings 17:21). From this followed the Samaritans' antagonism of the Jews at their return from captivity (Ezra 4; Nehemiah 4), which led to the erection of rival temples on Mount Gerizim. This is cited in the woman's statement to Jesus at the well (John 4:20), "Our fathers worshiped on this mountain." From that time on the spirit of religious bitterness lingered, and this accounts for the Jewish reproach. Unlike the Jews,

Jesus had dealings with the Samaritans. According to Luke 9:55-56 - 10:30-37, He spoke well of them, healed one of leprosy, and rebuked two Samaritans for asking permission to destroy some of their people with fire from heaven.

Jesus said it was necessary for Him to go through Samaria (John 4:4), and He knew all about the woman in Samaria as the omniscient Lord. He went there to show that He was above all religious and racial prejudices and that true worship consists of worshiping God in spirit and truth. Jesus traveled to Samaria with His disciples and, reaching Jacob's well, being tired and thirsty from the hot journey, rested by the well and sent His disciples into the city to buy food. Resting at the well, He met the woman, who was coming to carry water back to her abode. This is a hint to the woman's station in life, for women of affluence did not carry water in those times. Jesus had been waiting for her, and He knew the time of her arrival.

As she arrives and is drawing water, Jesus engages her in conversation by asking her for a drink of water. She is stunned and answers, "How is it that you, being a Jew, ask a drink from me, a Samaritan woman? For Jews have no dealings with Samaritans" (John 4:9). Jesus answers her in verse 10, "If you knew the gift of God, and who it is who says to you, 'Give Me a drink,' you would have asked Him, and He would have given you living water." The conversation continues between them, drawing answers about this woman's life.

The Samaritan woman has had five husbands and is now with a man who is not her husband, but her live-in lover. She has come to carry water from Jacob's well without male escort—not even the man she is currently with will do this for her. It is at a time when other women do not go to the well. She is known in the city and does not want to engage in conversation with other women for the shame of her known lifestyle. Yet Jesus has come to make her a new offer. He knows about her five husbands, He knows about her current lover, and He knows all that she has gone through trying to survive. He has not arrived to judge her or condemn her, nor to put her business in the streets.

It is just her and her God, unbeknownst to her, having a conversation—having her prayers answered. Jesus did not come in the midst of a crowd or with His disciples to confront her, but in the privacy of her daily chores. He says to her one thing, "Go, call your husband," and her truthful answer permits Him to tell her about her past life. She is amazed and declares He must be a prophet. She takes up the issue of where she and her fathers worshiped God, for they had been restricted (because of their mixed bloodline with the Assyrians) from mixing with those Jews who kept their bloodlines pure from intermarrying outside their religious lineage. This woman who was presently living in sin was looking for the Messiah, not knowing she was standing before Him, because in verse 25 she says, "I know that Messiah is coming" (who is called Christ). "When He comes, He will tell us all things." Jesus answers in verse 26, "I who speak to you am He."

Now the disciples return and are upset that Jesus is speaking with her, for their thoughts are revealed to Jesus in verse 27. But at this point the woman is so excited that she leaves her water pot and runs into the city to tell everyone, "Come see a Man who told me all things that I ever did. Could this be the Christ?" Imagine if you can this woman who did not want to run into other women at the well for fear of being rejected because of her present situation, now running off to testify to those in the city about the Messiah. Even more so, imagine that Jesus took the time to go through Samaria to see a woman who was living in shame and probably in emotional pain trying to survive after five husbands; she was now living with someone who did not even spare her the shame of going into the city to draw water so he could eat and wash and refresh himself. Only God knows what other treatment she endured to survive as a woman trying to make ends meet.

Jesus disclosed her five former husbands; we do not know whether they died one after the other (causing her to marry the brother of the deceased), but she was now living with a man who was not her husband. A man according to that time could have divorced her because she burnt his food, or for any reason if she did not please him. She may not have been the most beautiful woman, but at night or for a brief moment of pleasure they were able to put that aside. She endured all that and more possibly in hopes that one day she might meet a man who would see her heart and love her for the person she truly was—a good woman in a bad situation. A good woman trying to survive the best way she knew how without giving up on life, and praying for a better way.

This day her prayer was answered, and God did not send an angel to bring her a message of His love, mercy, and forgiveness. He did not ask one of the rabbis to go talk with her or a would-be prophet. But He, God manifested in the flesh, came to her at a well where she was thirsty and tired. He met her at the place of her need. Jesus desires to meet those women who are waiting for Him and looking for Him that He might tell them He has the water, the only water that will satisfy their thirst and the deepest longings of their soul. Everyone else may have promised her satisfaction and love, but only Jesus was capable of delivering it. It is most probable that her parents were dead and she had no brothers who would take responsibility for her care and protection, being left to the mercilessness of society.

One encounter with Jesus made her leave her water pot and the man waiting for her at home and go into the city to give the great news. She evangelized a city with the news of the Messiah. Jesus considers each woman, case by case, important enough to make a personal trip for, to let her know He loves her enough to come looking for her. He knows the longings of her heart. Jesus confessed something to her that He did not usually confess to others, not even His disciples. He said, "I am the Messiah." Her entire situation changed from that moment forth, and so will yours when you turn your situation over to Jesus!

CHAPTER EIGHT

THE ADULTEROUS WOMAN'S SITUATION
(John 8:1-11)

- Caught in the bed of a married man

- Brought before Jesus openly amid a crowd

- The crowd and the law say stone her

A WOMAN caught in the act of adultery, as the Scriptures refer to her, was the bait in a trap to get Jesus by the scribes and Pharisees. They knew where to go and what time to go there in order to catch her and the man in the act. Despite the law, they only brought the woman and never put the man on the spot. Jesus, having spent the night on the Mount of Olives, rose early the next morning to go to the Temple where a large company of people would gather to hear about His messianic work. Jesus knew the Sanhedrin was seeking an opportunity to condemn and judge Him so they could put Him to death, and this day they too gathered around Him. While He was seated in the Temple instructing the people, a number of the scribes and Pharisees arrived bringing with them a woman who had been caught committing a most degrading and serious offense. This act, according to Deuteronomy 17:2-7, was so serious it called for the stoning death of the man and woman involved.

The group that brought the woman to Jesus belonged to a class most eager to deal with harlots. They regarded themselves as custodians of public morality, and those who came under the observation of these inspectors would receive the full letter of the law in punishment. But they executed the law with partiality in some cases, this one particularly. For knowing the Law as they did, they did not bring the man whom she committed this act with. He seemed to have been excused while they dragged this poor woman out publicly. The Law and justice demanded that the adulterer and adulteress be brought together and put to death (Leviticus 20:10), but true to the way of the world those enemies of Christ made the woman bear the severity of her offense. Divine justice, however, is "without partiality" (James 3:17).

This woman was guilty beyond any shadow of doubt, and Jesus in no way condoned her sin or the seriousness of her offense. He pitied the woman's weakness and made full allowance for the force of temptation compelling her to sin. But we also see from His command to "go and sin no more" that He regarded her conduct as being a manifestation of wickedness. Yes, adultery takes its place in the front rank of "the works of the flesh" (Galatians 5:19) and is against the Creator's just and holy law regarding the welfare of the race (Exodus 20:14). But could there be anything crueler than to set this sinful woman in the center of the Temple, exposing her to the gazing eyes of the multitude and pious religious leaders? This is religion at its coldest level. It was bad enough for the woman to be conscious of her sin, but to parade her before others was a cruel act and destitute of the love eager to hide a multitude of sins (1 Peter 4:8). The conduct of those scribes and Pharisees displayed a cold, hard cynicism, void of any grace or pity, exposing barbarous brutality of heart and conscience.

Now in contrast to these cruel religious leaders we see Jesus, teaching us how to help reconcile those who have fallen to temptation. While we must understand that Jesus as the Messiah was under solemn obligation to respect the Law of Moses (Deuteronomy 31:9; Matthew 5:17), which in His life on earth He fulfilled (Matthew 5:18), we also must see that He does not judge by the law without love. Jesus shows God's love toward us, for He deals with us privately until we refuse to hear Him and take heed. Then He will finally deal with us publicly to help us repent and keep us in fellowship with Him.

The men quoted Moses to Jesus and asked Him what His judgment for such an act would be. They knew Jesus' kindness and hoped to trap Him. They recited that Moses said she should be stoned, "but what do You say about it, Jesus?" The devil was behind the Pharisees' effort to tempt and accuse Christ, and He needed wisdom to deal with such a situation. Being able to read men's hearts, He knew how to answer their question—and did so masterfully. He stooped and wrote in the dust around His feet, "as though he heard them not." Silence, how powerful it was, for it even enraged the men as He kept writing and they kept demanding an answer. He never looked upon the woman or their faces, but when He finally spoke, they probably wished He had remained silent, for they were convicted by His words: "Let him who is without sin among you cast the first stone."

The only one among them without sin was Jesus! As self-righteous as they were, they had to drop their stones and walk away.

After they leave, Jesus addresses the woman and asks her where her accusers are. She realizes they have left, and she hears the greatest words from our Lord—"neither do

I condemn you, go and sin no more." He forgives her and shows her love and kindness with compassion. So often the religious ones deal harshly and coldly with people who have fallen into sexual sins. Now, this is not to say that it should be taken lightly, but the Bible tells us we are to go to our brother or sister in the spirit of meekness. The point is to turn them back to the path of righteousness and God's direction, knowing that any other way leads to death and destruction. We don't want to lose a soul.

The woman's words to Jesus, in answer to His question, are "No man, Lord." She recognizes that He is the only one who has the right to pass judgment on her. She makes no attempt to defend or excuse herself. She calls Him Lord! Jesus' dealing with her leads her to receive Him as Lord! His love and treatment of her is holy and righteous in judgment. Yet He tells her to change, to no longer be a sinner for there is a better way, a better life that awaits her. He knows the reason for her sin and sees her heart, which the scribes and Pharisees failed to see. All they could think of was the law and how those who fail to keep it must be punished and pointed out—until it was their turn to be exposed.

This was the greatest day of this woman's life, for her sin brought her to the feet of Jesus, the one who loved her soul, her

Creator. From this day forward she would never be the same. There may still be some struggles and certainly temptations, but she found that the love of God would be her strength and help her to overcome the temptations of her flesh.

Conclusion

The apostle Paul wrote in Galatians 6:1-2, "Brethren, even if anyone is caught in any trespass, you who are spiritual, restore such a one in a spirit of gentleness, each one looking to yourself, so that you too will not be tempted. Bear one another's burdens, and thereby fulfill the law of Christ." It is my prayer that this book will be a tool of restoration, hope, and strength for women who have been directed by their situations and brought to shame, humiliation, low self-esteem, and discouragement.

The Scriptures teach that all of us have fallen short of the glory of God and at some point allowed a situation to cause us poor judgment in making a right decision. Perhaps some situations, which may have been out of one's control, placed him or her in a helpless position leaving a scarred self-image. Well, look and live, my sister, live! The ever abounding grace of God enables Him to wash you and cleanse you from all unrighteousness. It is time to give the negative opinions of others and yourself, along with your poor self-image, to Jesus Christ and let Him make you the "new creation" He desires to.

He delights to see you with renewed strength if you have fallen during your walk with Him. He desires that you get up and keep looking to Him, for He is the author and finisher of your faith. The lives of these women—Bathsheba, Tamar, Rahab, and the others—teach us a lesson about God and ourselves. Six of these women experienced that their situations could not hinder the blessings of God when they sought to change (repent) and do it His way—despite the situation, He blessed them. God understood their journey and the process, just as He understands yours. Only men look on the outward appearance, but God looks on the heart. Two of the women, Michal and Jezebel, did not seek God and allow Him to change not only their lives but their hearts, and therefore they suffered negative consequences to the end of their lives. The ending could have been different had they turned to Him and found that His judgments are altogether righteous and executed in love.

To all of those who know a so-called "bad" woman who may be struggling in a bad situation, show her the grace of God through your love and patience with her. Encourage her out of the bad situation that is keeping her bound, fast for her, pray for her, and war in the spirit for her. Do not judge her and give up on her; instead, show her the love of Christ in you by reaching out to her with compassion and under-standing—for it is the enemy who seeks to steal, kill, and destroy. But it is Jesus who has come to give life, and give it abundantly. Show her how valuable she is by the price Jesus paid for her forgiveness. Jesus said He is the same yesterday, today, and forever. The same God who showed grace to these women, those who sought Him in this book, is the same God who will show the contemporary women of these times His all-sufficient grace. There are many good women who find themselves in bad situations—some are in Christ and others are outside the faith, but we are sounding the alarm that *grace* awaits them. Receive it!

Endnotes

Chapter 1: Bathsheba's Situation

1. *Why We Love: The Nature and Chemistry of Romantic Love*, Helen Fisher (New York: Henry Holt, 2004), 75.
2. Ibid., 52.
3. Ibid., 53.

Chapter 2: Rahab's Situation

1. *All the Women of the Bible*, Herbert Lockyer (Grand Rapids: Zondervan Publishing House, 1983), 131.
2. *All the Trades and Occupations of the Bible*, Herbert Lockyer (Grand Rapids: Zondervan Publishing House, 1986), 272.

CPSIA information can be obtained at www.ICGtesting.com
Printed in the USA
BVOW020911230112

281053BV00001B/66/P